1.1 -

Moo Jim,

May we always make the time to treat children with love and respect for they are our future.

Warmly,

Sandra Joseph

A Voice for the Child

I am not here to be loved and admired,
But to act and love.
It is not the duty of people to help me,
But it is my duty to look after the world,
And the people in it.

JANUSZ KORCZAK

A Voice for the Child

The inspirational words of Janusz Korczak

EDITED BY

Sandra Joseph

Thorsons
An Imprint of HarperCollins*Publishers*

Thorsons
An Imprint of HarperCollins*Publishers*
77–85 Fulham Palace Road
Hammersmith, London W6 8JB

Published by Thorsons 1999

1 3 5 7 9 10 8 6 4 2

A catalogue record for this book
is available from the British Library

ISBN 0 7225 3806 5

Typeset by Harper Phototypesetters Limited,
Northampton, England
Printed and bound in Great Britain by
Woolnough Bookbinding Ltd, Irthlingborough

Contents

Acknowledgements

My heartfelt gratitude and thanks to Michele Pilley at Thorsons and her superb team of professionals, especially Charlotte Ridings. Michele, without your vision and dedication, this book would never have existed.

Thank you Felek Scharf for always being there for me. My thanks also to Itzhak Belfer and all the people at the Janusz Korczak Society in Israel, especially Dr. Shevach Eden and Benjamin Anolik.

There are no words to express the gratitude I feel towards Tamzin Lazarus. Thank you for sharing this journey with me.

A very special thank you to my dear friend Carole Lindey, who patiently gave me so much time, advice and encouragement.

And finally to my family. John, thank you for all your love, support and wisdom. Susie, Simon, Lance, Yifat and granddaughter Elle – thank you, for being who you are and for bringing so much joy into my life.

Illustrations by Itzhak Belfer
(one of Korczak's orphans)

Itzhak Belfer was born in Poland in 1923, and was brought up in the Janusz Korczak orphanage in Warsaw.

When Warsaw fell to the Germans, Belfer escaped through the Polish forests to Russia. After the war he returned to Warsaw and the cataclysmic extinction of the Polish Jewry.

In 1947, sailing to Israel as an illegal immigrant, he was captured by the British and interned in Cyprus, where he began painting the desolate winter prison camps.

Since 1948 he has lived in Israel, teaching art at the Tel Aviv University. His work has been exhibited worldwide.

Translated by
Theresa Prout
and
Anne Hargest Gorzelak

Preface

I hope that as a result of this book the English-speaking world will finally become familiar with Janusz Korczak and his work. Most of the quotes are taken from *How to Love a Child* and *Respect for the Child*, books he wrote over fifty years ago. But their insights and simple truths concerning children are as fresh and valuable today as they were then, for he was a man years ahead of his time.

How many of us go down the road of parenthood alone, unprepared and frightened of losing our way in the multitude of different theories and ideas on childcare that bombard us everyday? We are afflicted by guilt because we didn't do what this or that specialist says we should have. We become confused when points of reference move almost daily. There are hundreds of books on childcare – but they either concentrate on practical aspects or delve into areas of child psychology. How many of us need the simple inspiration and reassurance of being told, and revel in the words:

I do not know and there is no way for me to know
How parents unknown to me, can bring up a child unknown to me,
In circumstances which are also unknown.
I want everyone to understand that no book and no doctor

Is a substitute for your own intuition and careful observation.
No one can know your child as you do.

How often have we questioned children on some misdeed only to be confronted with a wall of silence? How comforted we would have been had we been guided by Korczak's simple wisdom:

The child is honest.
When he does not answer, he answers.
He doesn't want to lie, and he is too frightened to tell the truth.
To my surprise I have stumbled upon a new thought.
Silence is sometimes the highest expression of honesty.

By fate I fell into the world of Dr. Janusz Korczak whilst studying psychotherapy.

Bruno Bettelheim and Alice Miller, two of the world's foremost child psychotherapists, describe Korczak as one of the greatest educators of all times. I tried to find out more about this Dr. Korczak, especially his theories concerning education and child-care. At libraries I drew a blank. I asked teachers, social workers, therapists, everyone I knew, but nobody had heard of him. Finally, by a strange set of coincidences I was introduced to Felek Scharf, an expert on Polish affairs and one of the few living links with Korczak in the UK. He sat me down in his office and started talking about him.

This was the start of a journey that would change my life. He showed me two books by Korczak which had been translated into English. One was his famous children's book *King Matt the First*, and the other was his *Ghetto Diary*, written at the end of his life. 'But what about his work on children?' I asked. Sadly Felek shook his head. Very little had been published in English. I left with two treasured books: *How to Love a Child* and *Respect for the Child* by Janusz Korczak, but they were written in Polish. I felt so frustrated. Slowly the idea dawned on me that there was no way I could enter into his world until the books were translated into English. A year later a biography of Korczak came out by Betty Lifton called *The King of Children* and at the same time the film *Korczak*, directed by Poland's greatest film director Andrzej Wajda, was released. This convinced me even more.

I decided to do some research, and scanned through volumes of articles, newspaper cuttings and books to discover more about Korczak. The more I read the more enlightened and deeply moved I became as I learned of his life and work. He was not only an exceptional and original educator, he was a doctor, a philosopher, a great humanitarian, and a gifted writer whose works have received world-wide acclaim. There were so many different facets to his character and each shone brilliantly. It was difficult to separate the man from his work.

At last the translation was complete. I was amazed by what I read. He did not theorize, or give ready-made answers, but presented the fruits of his experience in such a clear simple way – almost like that of a child, direct but at the same time poetic, so that every reader could not help but be inspired. He became the guide on a journey inside the mind of a child, offering insights we all need to learn in our modern society in order to get back in touch with the child within us.

For over twenty years my professional life has been involved in working with children and young people. I knew through experience that all children want only one thing – to be loved, and respected. They have that right! They also have the right to be protected and cared for. They will then be able to show respect and care for others, contributing positively to our society. This is what Korczak stressed throughout his books. Again and again I kept asking myself the same question – Why isn't this man known?

I went to Israel to interview his 'children', now in their seventies and eighties – the few surviving orphans who are left. Their faces lit up when describing Korczak. He was a loved father to them all, at a time when they desperately needed one. They all spoke of the feeling of warmth, kindness and love they felt in his company; about his smiling blue eyes and great sense of humour. I asked how they would explain to people who knew nothing of Korczak, why the man was so important? One of them replied:

> It is difficult for me to explain to you in words the impact Korczak had on my life. He had so much compassion and a readiness to help all people. We used to say that Korczak was born to bring the world to redemption. What was so special about him was that he knew how to find a way to the child's soul. He penetrated the soul. The time spent at the orphanage formed my life. All the time Korczak pushed us to believe in other people and that essentially man is good. He was an innovator of the educational system – the first to reach the conclusion that the child had the same rights as the adult. He saw the child not as a creature who needs help, but as a person in his own

> right. All this was not just a theory – he applied it in our orphanage. There were no limitations in the framework of the rules. The child had the same rights as the teachers. For example, the Court's [the children's Court set up in the orphanage, where the children were judged by their peers] first mission was to protect the weaker child against the stronger. The rules were based in such a way that only children had the right to serve as judges. The teachers did all the paper work. When the war broke out and I was starving and ready to do anything, I didn't, because something of Korczak's teachings stayed with me.

I asked if history had been kind to Korczak or was he really a man like this – almost an angel? An elderly man with a broad smile answered:

> In my opinion this was his very nature. Maybe it was because he had witnessed such poverty and hardship among abandoned street children when he was a doctor that gave him the strength to dedicate all his life as he did. I cannot remember any negative side to Korczak's character, even now, when I myself am a grandfather and teacher, and understand more about children and their education. I honour the memory of a man who was my father for eight years; a man who has healed my physical and psychological ailments and who instilled a code of ethics that served me throughout my life.

I have shown Korczak's writings to young people, parents, teachers and anyone whose life is involved with children. They all encouraged me to pursue this book, validating the value of its message in today's world. However, it was the children I have counselled over the years, many of whom had experience of abuse and neglect, whose reaction surprised me the most. Without exception they all wanted to know more about Korczak and verified the truth of his basic theme – that all children want is to be loved and respected.

'If only my parents had read Korczak, they could have seen things from my point of view. Instead of feeling so isolated and misjudged, I could have quoted his words back to them. Maybe then they would have understood me.' They agreed with Korczak that every school would benefit from a Court of peers, which could help eradicate the ills of today's schools such as bullying and theft. They found it difficult to believe that, fifty years ago, he had set up a Committee (consisting of older children, himself and teachers) giving pupils a base to voice their ideas on improving the orphanage. They felt that if teachers listened to their opinions and valued their feelings in schools today, it would help minimize truancy by creating a happier and more democratic environment. Korczak always stressed the importance of 'learning from the child'.

Korczak deserves to be recognized and honoured today, not because he was a martyr, not because he was a great writer and doctor, not because he cared for the most neglected and poorest of children, not because he made a unique contribution to the world of education – but because he was a man of great humility, who lived and died solely because of his deep belief in and love for children. Korczak truly was 'The Champion of the Child'.

Sandra Joseph
September 1997

Be yourself and seek your own path.
Know yourself before you attempt to get to know children.
Become aware of what you yourself are capable of
Before you attempt to outline the rights and responsibilities of children.
First and foremost you must realize that you too are a child,
Whom you must first get to know, to bring up and to educate.

'I do not know' when used in science represents a nebula of theorizing,
From which emerge new insights approaching the truth.
'I do not know' for a mind not trained in scientific thinking is a frightening vacuum.
I want to teach people how to understand and love this miraculous, creative state of 'I do not know' when related to children –
So full of life and dazzling surprises!

Delinquency is the descendant of drunkenness, violence and insanity.
It does not echo any external voice, but obeys an inner call,
A sad moment, when the child realizes that he is different and difficult
That he is ostracized and cursed.
He looks for help – if he gets enough courage to trust someone.
He will seek refuge and ask, 'Can you save me?'
He confides his secret.
He wants to be better.

Children are not the people of tomorrow,
but are people of today.
They have a right to be taken seriously,
And to be treated with tenderness and respect.
They should be allowed to grow into whoever they were meant to be –
'The unknown person' inside each of them is our hope for the future.

The child has done something wrong, say he broke a window. He ought to be feeling guilty about it. But when we quite legitimately reprimand a child we rarely see remorse, but rather rebellion and a frowning, angry face. It is precisely when a child is guilty that he most needs the adult to show some sign of goodwill.

A broken window pane is nothing more than an unsuccessful undertaking, even if it had been attempted against our advice. And on top of the broken window, how are adults going to accept sulking and anger as well?

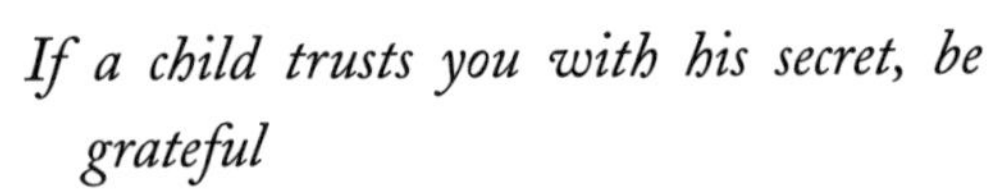

If a child trusts you with his secret, be grateful
For his confidence is the highest prize...
But do not extort it for the child has a right to his secret.
Do not plead or threaten, as each is equally bad.
It will not bring the child closer to you,
But rather move him away.

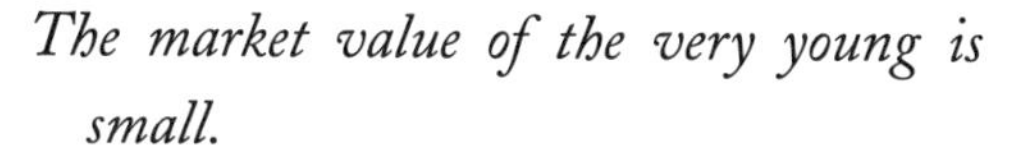

The market value of the very young is small.
Only in the sight of God is the apple blossom worth as much as the apple –
Green shoots as much as a field of ripe corn.

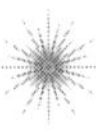

We burden the child with the duties of
men of tomorrow,
Without giving him any of the rights
of men of today.

I believe many children rebel against virtue
Because they have been incessantly trained
And overfed in its vocabulary.
Let the child discover for himself, slowly, the need of altruism,
Its beauty and its sweetness.

Children, let your dreams and aspirations
be proud.
Set your sights high.
Try to win glory.
Something will always come out of it.

If we are constantly astonished at the child's perceptiveness,
It means that we do not take them seriously.

I am filled with unbounded gratitude to this girl.
There is nothing special about her, nothing to attract attention,
An ordinary face, average mind, little imagination, absolute lack of
Tenderness.
Nothing that makes children adorable.
But it is nature, its eternal laws,
God, speaking through this unspectacular child,
Just as through any scrubby bush growing by the roadside.
Thank you, for being just as you are, just ordinary.

As for emotions, the child feels more strongly,
Having not yet developed inhibitions.
As for intellect, he is at least our equal,
Wanting nothing but experience.
That is why frequently an adult is like a child
And the child like an adult.
The only other difference is that he does not earn his keep,
And as a dependant is forced to submit to somebody else's will.

We treat adolescence as if the proceeding years had not also
Been stages of gradual growing to maturity,
Sometimes slowly, sometimes rapidly, in equal measure.
If we examine the weight curve we will have more understanding
For the tiredness, clumsiness, laziness, dreamy states, pallor, lack of
motivation and instability which characterizes this age.
Let us call it the age of 'The Big Unbalance'
Just to differentiate it from the previous ones.

Because a child cannot be idle, he will poke into every corner,
Inspect every nook and cranny,
Find things and ask questions about them.
Everything seems interesting to him.
The moving dot which turns out to be an ant.
The glittering glass bead or an expression or
Sentence which he may have overheard.
Think how much we are like children when we find ourselves
In a strange town or other unusual surroundings.

Mine

When you take away a spoon with which the child is banging the table
You are not depriving him of a possession but of a property
Which gives his hand the ability to get rid of energy,
Expressing itself in a different way by producing sound.
This hand, not quite his hand, but rather Aladdin's obedient genie
Can now hold a biscuit, gaining a new and valuable possession,
And the child will defend it.

To what extent does the concept of
possession tie up with the
Concept of enhanced power?
Primitive man discovered that his bow
and arrow were not merely a posses-
sion,
But a hand which could strike at a
distance.

Do children imitate? Of course they do.
But what does a traveller do when invited by an Eskimo
To take part in a local rite or ceremony?
He observes and tries not to stand out.
He attempts to catch the essence and relationship of the proceedings,
Feeling proud of himself at having played his part in them.

He seeks help when he cannot manage by himself.
When he attempts to do things independently, his efforts frequently come to nothing
And his dependency makes him impatient.
Even if he does not trust someone completely,
He must still let himself be guided by adults.
In the same way an invalid has to accept the help
and put up with the whims of an unsympathetic nurse.

It isn't what you play that is important – it is how you play
And what you think and feel when you are playing that matters.
You can play intelligently with a doll
And you can play a foolish game of chess.
You can use a great deal of imagination
And be totally absorbed in playing at being a policeman
A traindriver or a cowboy,
And you can read superficially and without interest.

A child talks in the language of gesture and he thinks in the language of images and emotional recall.
He understands speech, but not so much the words themselves as the gestures and tone of voice.
He stretches out his hands towards a desired object – 'Give it!'
He keeps reaching for something and finally with great effort succeeds in obtaining it.
He sighs deeply and with this sigh of relief he is saying 'At last!'
Now try and take it away from him and in ten different ways he will be telling you
'I will not give it up!'
He lifts his head, he sits, he stands up – 'I am doing things!'

And what does the smiling mouth and eyes communicate if not 'I am so happy to be alive!'

'Where is your nose?'
Without really understanding any of the words, simply from the tone of voice, the movement of the lips and the facial expresssion
He guesses what answer he is expected to give.
A baby can hold a very complicated conversation without being able to talk.

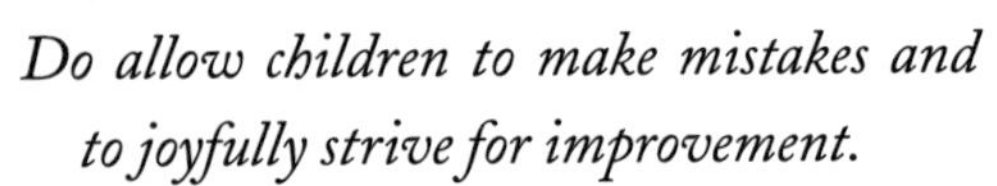

Do allow children to make mistakes and
to joyfully strive for improvement.
Children love laughter, running about
and playing tricks.
If your own life is like a graveyard to
you –
Leave children free to see it as a pasture.

Whenever I see a white-faced child playing with white toys, dressed in white clothes,
Surrounded by white furniture in a room decorated with white paint,
I have the unpleasant feeling that in this unchildish room,
More like a surgical ward,
A pallid soul will grow up in an anaemic body.

A child finds a prickly beard, a rough face and the smell of cigars offensive. He quickly wipes his face after every kiss, until he is told not to. Most children detest being sat on laps And when you take them by the hand they will gently, slowly try to remove it. All those senseless questions and laughter for no apparent reason. 'Who does she look like? Goodness how she has grown! What a sweet girl!' And the embarrassed child just stands there. When will it all end?

All children realizing my faults,
Would be glad to change me, to make me
better.
The poor youngsters cannot grasp
The fact that my greatest fault is that
I am no longer a child.

Dreams – Feelings which have no other
outlet flow into dreams.
A dream is a programme for life,
If only we knew how to decipher them
We would realize that dreams do come true.

A child can read his parent's face
In the same way as a farmer reads the sky
to predict the weather.

'When a grown-up spills some tea,
Mummy says "It's nothing"
But when I do it she gets angry!'
Children suffer acutely because they are unaccustomed to the pain of injustice.
They frequently cry and even their tears are treated as a joke or irritant
And made to seem unimportant.
'She is bawling, blubbering, whining again!'
A bouquet of words which adults invented for use against children.

The door is open at last and he heaves a great sigh of relief. This kind of deep sigh can be observed in even young babies following every effort of their will, or after a lengthy period of concentration. A child will sigh in a similar way when you finish telling him an interesting story. I am keen for everyone to be aware of this.

A deep solitary sigh like this is proof of the fact that the breathing which preceded it had been slowed down – almost held back. The child has been looking, waiting and observing with bated breath.

The child is not foolish,
There are no more fools among them than among adults.

We don't like it when children criticize us.
They are not permitted to notice our mistakes, or absurdities.
We appear before them in the garb of perfection
We play with children using marked cards
We win against the low cards of childhood with the aces of adulthood.
Cheaters that we are, we shuffle the cards in such a way that we deal ourselves everything.

How often do we feel disappointment, when children fail to live up to our expectations,
And how often do we feel disappointment at every step of their development?
We are their harsh judges, rather than their counsellors and consolers.

Under identical clothes
Beat a hundred different hearts,
And each one is another difficulty
Another task
Another worry and care.

There are new-borns and infants who cry very little. All the better.
But there are also some whose veins swell on the forehead when they cry
The top of the tiny skull becomes tense, purple spreads over the face and head
The lips become blue, the toothless jaw moves convulsively
The belly becomes screwed up and the hands draw tight into fists
The legs beat the air
Suddenly it stops, exhausted, with an expression of complete surrender on its face
It gazes at the mother 'reproachfully', blinks begging for sleep
But after a few rapid gasps, a similar and perhaps even stronger attack starts over again.
Can those tiny lungs, the little heart and the young brain possibly withstand all that strain?

A child with a vice feels it as a burden
But is at a loss what to do
Unless he has guidance
He will make a few disastrous attempts to change
And, after failing, will give up.

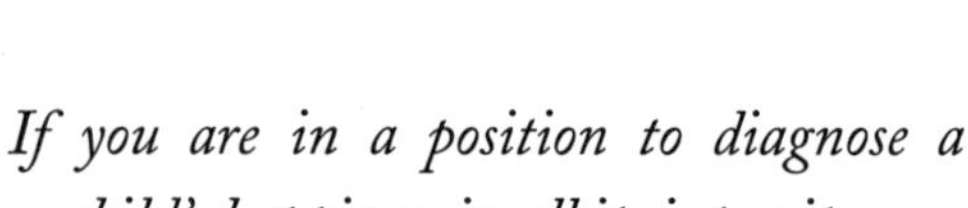

If you are in a position to diagnose a child's happiness in all its intensity
Then you cannot fail to notice that the highest level of joy
Results from having overcome some obstacle –
From a goal attained or a mystery solved
This is the happiness of triumph and the bliss of independence.

A child – a skilled actor –
Wears a hundred masks and plays a hundred different parts,
He acts differently with his mother, father, grandmother or grandfather,
With a strict or lenient teacher, with the rich or poor,
With his own friends.
Naïve and cunning, humble and haughty, gentle and vengeful
Well behaved and wilful,
He performs so well that he can lead us by the nose.

He must be given the freedom to drink his cup of happiness and to trust us
This is exactly what the child wants
Don't begrudge him time for a story, a game of ball,
Painting a picture together or copying the alphabet.
Give your time with patience and kindness.
The child is really right in expecting this.

Children are different from adults –
They may lack some things,
But they also have more of other things in
their lives than we have in ours.

*

There seems to be two kinds of existence.
One serious and respectable
The other indulgently tolerated and some-how less valuable.
We use expressions like 'Man of the future'
Implying by this that the child 'will be'.
Children make up a large proportion of humanity, of the population of the nation
They are our constant companions
They are here now
They always have been and they always will be.

*

We demand respect for a pair of bright eyes
A smooth brow and youthful effort and reliance.
Why should a dull look, a wrinkled brow, coarse grey hair and stooping resignation
Be more worthy of respect?
The same goes for the sunrise and the sunset,
It applies equally to the morning and the evening prayer.
A new generation is growing up and a new wave is rising
They are coming carrying their faults and virtues.

And we must give them the opportunity to grow up to be better,

We cannot win our case by simply lamenting over bad heredity.

We cannot just tell cornflowers to transform themselves into corn.

We are not miracle workers, but neither do we want to become charlatans.

We are relinquishing our hypocritical longing for perfect children.

We demand the following: eliminate hunger, abuse, cramped and overcrowded conditions, exploitation and the effects of war.

A delinquent child is still a child
That must not be forgotten for an instant
He has not given up yet,
Still does not know why he is what he is.
At times he realizes with alarm his own
separateness,
His being different from others.

Ungrateful

Is the earth grateful to the sun for shining on it?

Is the tree grateful to the seed that it grew out of?

Does the nightingale sing to his mother, thanking her that she used to keep him warm with her breast feathers?

Do you make a gift to the child of everything which you have received from your parents

Or do you only lend it to him in order to take it back again, writing everything down carefully and calculating the amount of interest due?

Is love a favour for which you demand remuneration?

'But is he clever?'

If the mother anxiously asks this question right from the start,

It will not take long before she will be placing demands on him.

It is not acceptable to well-to-do parents that their child will become a manual worker.

Rather, let him grow up unhappy and disheartened.

All this amounts to is not love for the child, but the parent's egotism

Not the happiness of the individual, but group ambition

Not a search for the best road in life, but shackles imposed by social convention.

You will never understand children
if you belittle their qualities.

There are one hundred more days left till spring. There is, as yet, not a blade of grass, not one single bud is showing. But inside the soil, among the roots, the dictate of spring is already there, secretly persisting, throbbing, lurking, waiting and gathering strength – under the snow, inside the bare branches, in the icy gale – to suddenly burst into blossom.

What a fever, a cough, or nausea is for the doctor,
So a smile, a tear or a blush should be for the teacher.
Medicine is concerned only with curing the sick child,
But an educator could nurture the whole child.
She could be the 'sculptor of the child's soul'.

Misdeeds and bad behaviour may require nothing more
Than patient, friendly understanding.
Delinquents need love.
Their angry rebellion is often just.
One should have little sympathy for easy virtue
But instead ally oneself with the lonely, cursed delinquent.
When, if not now, is he likely to receive the gift of our flourishing smile?

Painfully, the child shares the family's financial worries, compares his own poverty with a friend's affluence and suffers from the knowledge that he is helping to impoverish the family by simply being there.

He does not wish to be a burden.

There are many terrible things in this world
But the worst is when a child is afraid of his father, mother or teacher.
He fears them, instead of loving and trusting them.

Beware. Contemporary life has shaped a powerful brute – homo rapax.
It is he who dictates the mode of living.
His concessions to the weak are a lie.
His respect for the aged, for women's rights and kindness toward children are falsehoods.
Feelings are outcast like Cinderella.
It is really children who are the princes of feelings, the poets and thinkers.
We should respect with humility the white, bright, holiness of childhood.

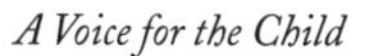

Life is a fairy tale.

In the sea there are fish that swallow people. If a fish swallows a man does he suffocate?

Why do fish have cold blood? Bees have a queen, but why is there no king. Is he dead?

If birds find their way to Africa, then they are cleverer than people are, because they never went to school. Why is it called a centipede when it does not really have a hundred legs and anyway, how many does it have then? Are all foxes cunning, and is there no chance of them reforming? Does a dog remain faithful, even when he is being tormented and beaten? Were stuffed animals once alive and can one stuff a human being? Why does it not hurt when a snake changes its skin? If you destroy a spider's web, will it die and where is it going to find another piece of thread to make a new web?

It is really true that a parrot understands nothing of what it says and is it more intelligent than a dog and why can't a dog have an operation done to his tongue so he can speak too? A tree is alive, it breathes and it dies. From a little acorn an oak tree grows. A flower turns into an apple – can one see it happening?

So what is a dragon compared to all this? He does not exist, but he could. How could St. George kill a dragon if they do not exist? And if mermaids do not exist, why are there pictures of them?

A cruel but legitimate law of Greece and Rome allowed children to be killed.

In the Middle Ages, fishermen would find bodies of drowned babies in their nets.

In 18th century Paris, in front of Notre Dame, older children were sold to beggars and younger ones were given away for nothing.

Not so very long ago.

Even today, in some parts of the world, children are abandoned if they happen to get in the way.

The number of illegitimate, neglected, abused, exploited, deprived and maltreated children is increasing all the time.

It is true that they are protected by law, but is this protection adequate? Old laws need to be revised.

The child's thinking is neither more limited nor inferior to that of an adult.
It is different.
The child thinks with feelings and not with the intellect.
That is why communication is so complicated
And speaking with children is a difficult art.

At last a mother's face ceases to be a mere shadow,
As by now it has been carefully explored by his hands.
Over and over again the baby catches her by the nose,
Touches her eyes, such strange objects
Alternating between appearing shiny when open and then lustreless when closed.
He examines her hair and pries her mouth open with his fingers in order to examine her teeth and look in her mouth with the utmost concentration and gravity.
The only things which stand in his way are the chatter, the kisses, jokes and all the things which we refer to as 'playing' with the baby.
Already at this stage he possesses certainties, assumptions and problems related to the investigations which he is conducting.

It has been said that a child, in his constant search for new feelings and impressions,

Finds it difficult to occupy himself with anything for long.

Games quickly become boring and a friend of one hour ago may now be an enemy,

Only to become a dear friend again a few minutes from now.

But I have ample proof that a child is capable of being involved in a single activity for weeks and months on end, without desiring change.

A particular toy never seems to lose its charm.

He will listen to the same fairy tale many times over, with the same rapt attention.

I also have proof to the contrary; that it is parents who become impatient with the monotonousness of the child's interests. In the same way they assume he cannot enjoy eating porridge and stewed fruit all the time.

People speak of the old with weighty respect.
They speak of the child patronizingly and condescendingly.
This is wrong, for the child too deserves respect.
He is still small, weak.
He does not know much, he cannot do much as yet.
But his future – what he will be when he grows up
Commands us to respect him as we respect the old.

Having experienced a number of improper questions
Unsuccessful jokes and betrayed confidences,
The child learns to look upon adults as wild animals, seemingly tamed
But who can never really be trusted.

Nobility of spirit cannot be a morning mist,
It has to take the form of a shaft of light.
If we are not up to it just yet
Let us at least bring up honest individuals.

A child only attracts our attention when she disrupts or disturbs us
We only take notice of and remember those instances.
We do not notice her in her quiet, serious and concentrated mood
We ignore the mystical moments when she converses with herself
With the world and with God.
Forced to conceal her feelings of longing or elation
For fear of evoking ridicule and scolding
The child controls her desire to communicate.
Obediently she hides her keen, surprised, or anxious expressions,
Her angry and rebellious feelings.
We expect her to dance and clap her hands
So she presents us with a clown's grinning face.

You say 'He ought to … I want him to…'
And you look for a pattern for him to follow
And you search for a life which you wish
him to have.

How often do we groan about the mess in a child's room? But should we not be turning our attention and research in this direction? Perhaps what is really needed is a large heap of yellow sand, a substantial bundle of sticks and a box full of stones. It may well be that a piece of wood, some cardboard, a pound of nails, a saw, a hammer and a lathe would make a much more welcome gift than a 'game' and an instructor in handicrafts might be more useful than a gymnastic or piano teacher. But then it would also become necessary to do away with clinical hygiene and the fear of a cut finger!

A mother's burning love for her child
Must also give him the right to an early death and the ending of his life cycle.
Not necessarily at the end of seventy odd earth's journeys around the sun,
But perhaps after only one, two or three springtimes.
'The Lord giveth and the Lord taketh away', says the natural scientist
Who knows that not every seed germinates.
Not every fledgling born is capable of staying alive
And not every bush grows into a tree.

Dear Lord, I stand before Thee in all humility, but the request I put before Thee is a burning desire. I proclaim my petition, as I stand before Thee, driven as I am by a relentless will, although I whisper these words. I am projecting my commanding glances above the clouds.

I stand erect as I make my demands, for they are not for myself. Bless the children, their endeavours and their strivings. Lead them through life's journey, not by the easiest, but by the most beautiful road.

I offer sadness, the only precious thing I own, as an offering. Sadness and work.

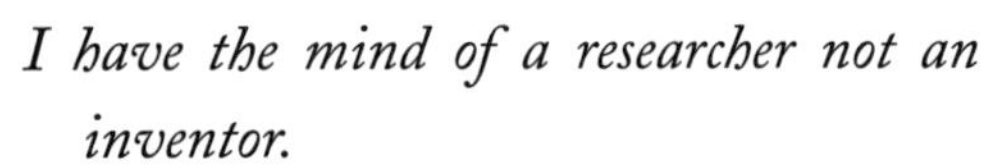

I have the mind of a researcher not an inventor.
To study in order to know? No.
To study in order to know more? No, again.
I think it is to study in order to ask more and more questions.

A hundred children – a hundred people
Who are not 'maybe sometime',
Not 'not now', not 'tomorrow'
But are here and now, today
People who already exist.

You already know that you do not know
Things are not what you have thought, so they must be different.
Without realizing it, you are already searching for the right track.
Feeling lost?
Remember that it is no shame to be lost in the great jungle of life.
Though you may stray, keep on looking around keenly
And you will see a mosaic of beautiful images.
You are suffering?
In pain, truth is born.

A child knows his environment; its moods, habits and failings.

He knows it and, one should add, he exploits it skilfully.

He can intuit kindness, detect deceit and has a sense of the ridiculous.

He is able to read a face, in the same way a farmer reads the sky to forecast the weather.

This is because he too has been observing and investigating us for many years.

A human being is responsible for his own
spirit and his own thoughts
Because they constitute his workshop.

A plea on behalf of respect for the here and now, for today.
How can we assure life in the future,
If we have not yet learned how to live consciously
And responsibly in the present?
Do not trample, hold in contempt
Or sell the future into bondage.
Do not stifle it, rush or force it.
Respect every single moment, as it will pass
And will never again be repeated.
If you maim it, it will bleed
And if you kill it, it will haunt you with its spectre of terrifying memories.

We are brought up with the idea that anything big is worthier than anything small.

It is unpleasant to stand on tiptoe and still not be able to reach anything.

The little steps cannot keep up with the grown-ups.

The tumbler keeps slipping out of the tiny hand.

Clumsily, only with the greatest effort, does he manage to climb onto the chair, or up the stairs.

He finds it hard to reach a doorknob or to look out of the window.

Everything seems to be too high up!

No notice is taken of him in a crowd.

His view is blocked and people keep bumping into him.

It is a nuisance to be small!

Everything that is big and takes up more room is respected and admired.

What is small is mundane and of little interest.

This applies equally to small people, small needs, small joys as well as small sorrows.

Among the things which impress everyone are big cities, high mountains or a lofty tree.

We say: 'A great deed', 'A great man'.

The child is small – there is just less of him.

We ought to stoop and come down to his level.

What a powerful effect on the sad life of a child,
Would be the memory of that person – perhaps the only one –
Who showed kindness, understanding and respect
In a world where cruelty had become the norm.
The child's future life and sense of himself could take a different course,
Knowing there was one person who would not fail him.

You must learn to trust your own perceptions,
For no one can know your child as you do.
To demand that others should provide you with all the answers,
Is like asking a strange woman to give birth to your baby.
There are some insights that can only be born out of your own pain,
and these often turn out to be the most valuable.
I want everyone to understand that no book, no doctor,
Is a substitute for your own sensitive intuition and careful observation.

You say 'My child.'
When if not during your pregnancy do you have more right to say this?
The beating of the tiny heart, no bigger than a peach stone, echoes your own pulse.
Your breath also provides him with oxygen.
The blood courses through you both
And no drop of the red blood quite knows yet
Whether it will remain yours or become his,
Whether it will be spilt and die in the tribute exacted by the mystery of conception and birth.

Every bite of bread which you eat becomes material for building his legs
On which he will run about,
For his skin which will cover him,
For his eyes with which he will see,
For his brain in which thoughts will burst into flame,
For the arms which he will stretch towards you
And for the smile with which he will call you 'Mummy'.

*

You shall live through this decisive moment together,
You will suffer the same pain together.
The bell will finally strike with the password:
– It is ready.

At the same time he will say 'I want to live my own life.'
You will eject him with the aid of powerful visceral cramps oblivious to his pain
And he will force his way out, oblivious to your pain.
A brutal act.

*

No, both you and the child will transmit a hundred thousand
Imperceptible, subtle, amazingly skilful vibrations,
Which will make sure that neither of you takes over more than your allotted area of life,
No more than is due to you,
And only that which is allocated to you by the universal law.

'My child'
No, not even during the many months of
pregnancy or during the birth,
Does the child really belong to you.

The child you have given birth to weighs ten pounds.
He consists of eight pounds of water, a handful of carbon, some calcium, nitrogen, sulphur, phosphorus, potassium and iron.
You have given birth to eight pounds of water and two of ashes.
And every drop within this child of yours had once been vapour in a cloud, a snow crystal, mist, dew, spring water or the drudge in the city's sewers.
Every atom of the carbon and nitrogen had once been bound up with some chemical compound.
All you did was to collect everything which already existed.

The earth is suspended in infinity.

A close friend, the sun, is fifty million miles away.

The diameter of this small earth of ours is only three thousand miles of fire, covered with a thin, coagulated shell only ten miles thick.

And on top of this thin shell filled with fire, amongst the oceans, a handful of dry land is scattered.

And on this dry land, amongst the trees and shrubs, insects, birds and animals, people can be seen swarming around.

Among all these millions of people you have given birth to one more – is that not so?

So another child is born – a trifle, a speck of dust, a bit of nothing. It is so fragile that it could easily by wiped out by a germ which is only just visible to the naked eye when magnified a thousand times. However, this bit of nothing is the flesh and blood brother to the ocean wave, to the wind, to lightning, to the sun and to the Milky Way. This speck of dust is brother to a sheaf of corn, to the grass, to an oak tree, to a nestling, a lion cub, a foal or a puppy.

Everything can already be found there; he feels, investigates, suffers, desires, experiences joy, love, trust, faith, hate, belief, doubt. He knows how to embrace and how to reject. This speck of dust will be able to grasp everything; the stars and oceans, the mountains and precipices. And what else can the essence of the soul be, if not the whole universe, but without bounds. This is the contradictory nature of human beings, who have arisen from dust, but in whom God has set up residence.

You say 'My child.'
No, the child belongs jointly to the mother, the father, the grandparents and the great-grandparents.
Somebody's distant 'I' which remained dormant in several ancestors,
A voice emerging from a decayed, long forgotten tomb,
Suddenly speaks again in your child.

A child is a piece of parchment,
Which has been thoroughly covered with minute hieroglyphics,
Only a very small part of which will you ever be able to decipher.
At best you will manage to erase or simply cross out a few of them
And to replace them with your own contribution.
This is a law of nature.
Actually it is wonderful!
In every one of your children it is the first link in the immortal generation chain.
Try and find your own dormant particle in your unknown child.
Perhaps you will succeed in finding it, and even manage to develop it.

A child and boundlessness
A child and eternity.
A child – a speck of dust in space.
A child – a moment in time.

How can one anticipate the future and offer protection?
He is like a butterfly hovering above the raging torrent of life.
How can one imbue him with toughness without encumbering his lightness in flight,
How to temper him without wetting his wings?
What about with one's own example, help, advice and words?
But what if he rejects them all?
In fifteen years' time his gaze will be fixed into the future,
Whilst yours will be looking to the past.
You will be filled with memories and habits
And he with change and hope.
You are full of doubt,
He is expectant and full of trust.
You are anxious,

He is fearless.
When it is not ridiculing, cursing or being contemptuous of something,
Youth invariably wants to change the imperfect past.
This should be so.
Let him search but without blundering.
Let him climb high but without falling.
Let him clear the ground but without bloodying his hands.
Let him struggle, but carefully, carefully.
He will say:
'I don't agree with you. I have had enough of supervision. Don't you trust me?'

*

'So you do not need me any more?
Is this love of mine nothing but a burden to you?'

Bringing up a child is not an amusing pastime
But a job that requires a great deal of effort and hard work, as well as sleepless nights.
But do not give up these nights
for they will give you something that no book, no advice ever will.
Their value is not so much in imparting knowledge
As in bringing about a profound spiritual upheaval.
It is during the course of these nights that a wonderful ally,
The child's guardian angel may come into existence –
Namely the intuition of the maternal heart, a kind of clairvoyance,
Which you will learn to trust, for it will always speak the truth.

When is the proper time for a child to start walking?
When she does.
When should his teeth start cutting?
When they do.
How many hours should a baby sleep?
As long as she needs to.

A hundred babies. I lean over each cot.
Among them are those who are only a few weeks old,
Of varied weights, with different histories.
Some are sick, others convalescent, still others healthy
And some are barely managing to hang on to their lives.
I come in contact with many different sorts of gazes,
Ranging from dimly clouded, without any expression,
To those which are lively, cheerful and provocative.
And the smiles can also vary, from welcoming, spontaneous and friendly
To ones which will appear only after several minutes of careful observation
Or in response to a smiling face or the stimulus of an endearing word.

Where could she have caught this cold?
Could it have been avoided?
Can it be that this minor infection makes her more resistant against another, more virulent one
Which she may come in contact with next week or next month?
Does it not perhaps strengthen the defence mechanism?
Can we isolate children from the air they breathe,
Containing thousands of bacteria in each cubic centimetre?

Can it be that children's interest in and liking for their shoes
Stems from the fact that they associate them with their ability to walk?
In the same way the child's coat becomes the fairytale magic carpet,
Which is able to carry the child into the fairyland of a walk outside.

He is inexperienced.

He drops a glass on the floor.

Then something extraordinary happens.

The glass has disappeared and completely different objects have appeared in its place!

He leans over, picks up a piece of glass, cuts his finger which begins to bleed.

Everything is full of mysteries and surprises.

The child must be seen as a foreigner,
Who does not speak our language
And who is ignorant of the laws and customs.
Occasionally she likes to go sightseeing on her own
And when lost will ask for information and advice.
Wanted – a guide to answer questions politely and patiently.
Treat her ignorance with respect.

Children want to see, verify and experience everything,
Although much remains which they will just have to take on trust.
People say 'There is only one moon.'
But how can one moon be seen from everywhere?

*

'Listen, I will stand on the other side of the fence and you stay in the garden.'
They close the gate.
'Well, can you see the moon from the garden?'
'Yes'
'I can see it from here as well!'
They change places and check again,
And now they are quite certain that there are really two moons!

The child is honest. When he does not answer, he answers.
For he doesn't want to lie and he cannot say the truth.
To my surprise, I have stumbled on a new thought.
Silence is sometimes the highest expression of honesty.

I should like to mention here the mutual love of parents. It is true the child seldom senses the lack of it when it is not there, but he does absorb it when it is.

We don't like it when a child who has just been scolded, keeps mumbling something under his breath,
Because in his anger, he might let slip what he really thinks of us.
Which we may not be too keen to hear.

A child brings a marvellous poetic silence into his mother's life.
The rhythm and nature of her life will depend on the many hours she spends with him,
When he is not demanding attention, but just being.
The thoughts with which she envelops him, in quiet contemplation,
Will inspire her to mature together with her child,
To accomplish the work necessary in bringing him up.
Her inspiration will not come from books, but from deep within herself.
Then every book she reads will be considered of little value;
And this one too, will have fulfilled its purpose if it has brought home this idea.
Just remember to be aware in your quiet solitude.

The adult often casts a reluctant eye on the contents of a child's pockets and drawers. One can find almost everything there, including pictures, postcards, pieces of string, nails, pebbles, bits of material, beads, boxes, bits of coloured glass, stamps, birds' feathers, fircones, conkers, ribbons, dried leaves and flowers, paper cut-outs, bus tickets, leftover bits of things which no longer exist and the nuclei of things just being created. Every little object has its history and a particular source of origin. These may be remembrances of things past, as well as longings for things to come.

A small shell may represent a dream of a trip to the sea.

A screw and a few bits of wire – an aeroplane and dreams of flying.

A doll's eye, broken long ago – the only keepsake of a lost love.

One is also likely to find there a photo of mother or father wrapped in a piece of tissue, or a coin – a present from a loved grandfather who has passed away.

Unfortunately, sometimes in anger or in a bad mood, the insensitive adult makes a heap out of these treasures and throws them away, because they are damaging pockets and jamming drawers. How heartless to treat other people's property in this way. How can one expect the child to have respect for anything or anyone? It is not bits of paper that end up in the dustbin, but cherished belongings and dreams of a wonderful life.

Respect for the mysteries and the ups and downs of that difficult task of growing up.
Respect for the here and now, for the present.
How will she be able to get on in life tomorrow,
If we are not allowing her to live a conscious, responsible life today?
Respect for every moment,
Because each will pass and never return.

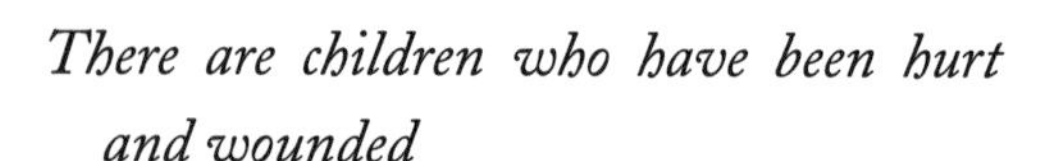

There are children who have been hurt and wounded
Some have clean wounds, which do not leave behind any scars
And these tend to heal of their own accord under a clean dressing.
However, one needs to wait longer for the wounds produced by clawing to heal
As these do leave behind painful scars.
One should avoid touching these, as they demand more care and patience.
People say, 'He is on the mend.'
How one would like to include the soul in this statement as well.

In the world of feeling, children are much richer.
They think with their emotions.

A poet is someone who is very happy and very sad,
Who is quick to anger and who loves intensely,
Who feels strongly, and who sympathizes with others' feelings.
Children are like that too.
A philosopher is someone who is very observant, who ponders
And wants to know how things really are.
Children are like that too.
It is hard for children to say what they are feeling
Or what they are thinking about,
Because speech requires words.
It is harder still for them to write,
But children truly are philosophers and poets.

We neither allow children to criticize us
Nor do we impose any controls over our-
selves.
We have renounced any attempts at self-
improvement
Instead we have burdened children with
this task.
The teacher also adopts this adult privi-
lege,
Which gives him license to supervise the
children, but not himself
To keep records of the children's transgres-
sions, but not of his own.
Do we try and make an effort to get on
better together?
Can it be that it is we who are stubborn?

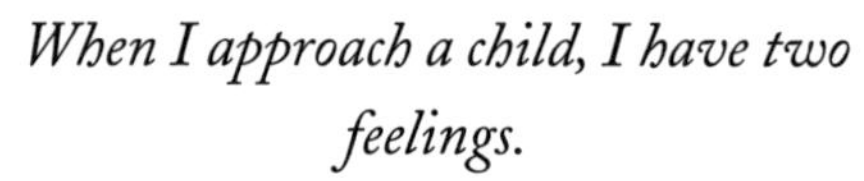

When I approach a child, I have two feelings.
Affection for what he is today
And respect for what he can become.

Why it is difficult to find a common language with children
Is that though they use the same words as we do,
They fill them with an entirely different content.
My *garden, father, death are not* his *garden, father, death.*

The spirit feels nostalgia in the narrow cage of the body.
Man ponders over death as the end,
But death is merely the continuation of life, another life.
You may not believe in the existence of the soul,
Yet you must acknowledge that your body will live on as green grass, as a cloud.
For you are, after all, water and dust.

The soul of a child is as complicated as ours,
And is full of similar contradictions in its perennial struggle –
I want to do it, but I can't. I know I should, but I just cannot manage it.

We are brothers, children of the same earth.
We have been preceded by generations that shared a common destiny
For good and for evil – one long common path.
We get light from the same sun and our crops are destroyed by the same hail
The same earth covers the bones of our forefathers.
We have known more sorrow than joy, more tears than laughter
And neither you nor we bear the blame for this.
Let us all work together, let us educate ourselves together.

I have noticed that only fools insist that all human beings should be alike.
The wise are glad that in the world there is day and night, summer and winter, old and young
That there are butterflies in the garden and birds in the sky
That the flowers and the eyes of people come in different colours
That God, who created humans, created them male and female.
Only those who do not like to think are grieved by difference
And irritated by the variety that compels us to think, to see and to understand.

Trust your own perceptions
Each person carries an entire world with-
in himself
Everything exists twice – once the way it is
And the other the way he perceives it with
his own eyes and feelings.
You must dream your own dreams
But be ready to accept life as it is.
One day is happy and one day is sad
Sometimes you are successful and some-
times you are not
Sometimes the sun is shining and some-
times it is raining.
So what are the rules of life?
Each person must find out for himself.
What can one do?
The secret is not to get discouraged about
mistakes and to be honest.
He who is sincere, who pursues justice and
is considerate of another,
Is the one best loved by everyone.

Sickness in the family draws the child nearer.
There is something about such times parents and
Children alike refer to with warmth.

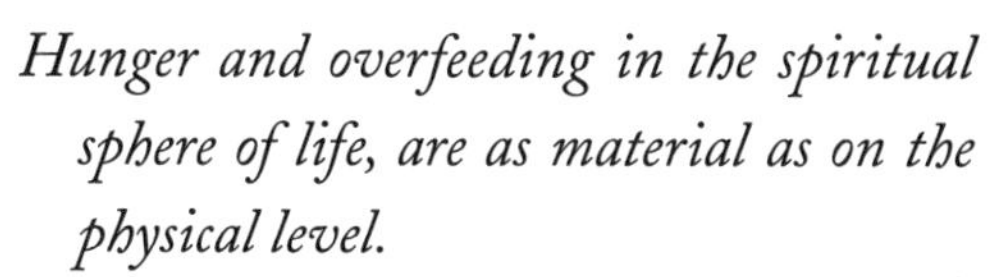

Hunger and overfeeding in the spiritual sphere of life, are as material as on the physical level.

A child hungry for advice and direction will absorb it, digest it and assimilate it.

Overfed with moral rules the child will suffer from nausea.

A good child.

One must be careful not to confuse a good child with an easy one.

He cries very little, he sleeps through the night, confident and good natured.

He is a good child.

Contemporary educational ideas strive to make the child more convenient to handle

And consequently attempt, step by step, to put to sleep, to stifle and to destroy

Everything which constitutes the child's will and freedom – the things which temper his spirit,

Which makes up the driving force behind his demands and intentions.

He is well-behaved, obedient, good, convenient,

But no consideration is given to the fact that his inner life may be indolent and stagnant.

Nothing but ignorance can make us over-
look the fact
that a baby has a certain, clearly defined
individuality,
Which is composed of inborn temperament,
strength, intellect, self-consciousness
And his life experiences.

What is this half of humanity which is living with us and alongside us in a state of tragic separateness?
We burden them with responsibilities belonging to people of the future,
But we fail to grant them any of the rights of citizens of today.

If we were to divide humanity into adults and children
And life into childhood and adulthood,
Then there would be very many children in the world and in life.
Being totally preoccupied with our own struggles and worries,
We do not take much notice of them,
Just as in former times the voices of women were not heard.

We have arranged things in such a way that children disturb our peace as little as possible.
We barely allow them a chance to speculate on what we actually are
And what we really do.

'I'.

When he tests the water in the bath and finds himself to be a conscious drop among all other unconscious drops, it is then that he apprehends the important truth contained in the short word 'I'.

We wish to seek some sign of the future.
But this anxious looking to what might be
distorts our view of what is.

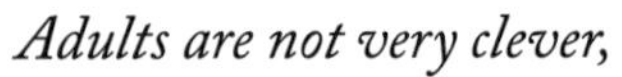

Adults are not very clever,
They do not even know how to take advantage of the freedom they have.
They are so lucky – they can buy anything they like,
They are allowed to do anything they want.
Despite all this they often get angry about something,
And any little thing is liable to make them shout.

Adults do not know everything.
They frequently answer without thinking just to get rid of you, or they make a joke.
One will tell you one thing, another something else
And it is impossible to tell who is telling the truth.
How many stars are there in the sky?
How do you say exercise book in African?
Is water alive?
How does it know when it is zero degrees centigrade that it has to turn into ice?

It must be remembered that a child's success does not depend exclusively on how adults judge him,
But equally, and perhaps in greater measure, on the opinion of other children of his own age.
They have a different set of rules governing the assessment of merit
And the granting of rights to the members of their community.

Forcing children to sleep when they are not sleepy is a crime.
A chart which proclaims when and how many hours a child is supposed to sleep is an absurdity.
It is easy to determine how many hours of sleep a child needs
By how many hours he tends to sleep without waking up.
There are periods when a child requires more sleep than normal
And there are others when he wants to lie awake in his bed, for he might be feeling tired
But not sleepy.

The principle of early to bed, early to rise (it matters little whether it is right or wrong)
Has been distorted by parents into something quite different for their own convenience:
the more sleep, the better it is for her health.

A summer camp for street children – sunshine, forests, rivers.
They are absorbing joy and goodness.
Yesterday's small tyrant becomes today's caring team member.
The shy, slow ones become bold, lively and full of initiative.
Here one can observe changes from one hour to the next, from week to week.
This does not mean that a miracle has taken place. No.
But that which was there in the first place was waiting to emerge.
Nothing is there which was not there before.

One is struck by the fact that everywhere military spending is greater than that for education. That metal costs more than future citizens, future human beings. This situation can be observed throughout the whole civilized world, with only small differences in scale evident.

We plunder the mountains, cut down the trees and destroy the animals.
More and more the forests and marshes are being replaced by settlements.
We are planting human beings in ever new territories –
We have subdued the world.

Politicians and legislators make rules and decisions about children, which often fail to work.
But who asks the child for his opinion or consent?
Who is likely to take note of any advice or approval from such a naïve being?
What can a child possibly have to say?

Alongside the children whose lives are like fairy-tales,
Who are trusting, friendly and happy,
There is a majority to whom, from their earliest days,
The world teaches the gloomy facts of life in plain, harsh words:
Poverty, abuse, neglect and indifference corrupt them.
They become angry, distrustful, withdrawn and resentful –
But not bad!

'Unfortunately I can give you nothing but these few poor words.
I cannot give you God, for you must find Him in quiet contemplation, In your own soul.
I cannot give you a Homeland, for you must find it in your own heart.
I cannot give you love of Man, for there is no love without forgiveness,
And forgiving is something everyone must learn to do on his own.
I can give you but one thing only –
A longing for a better life; a life of truth and justice: even though it may not exist now, it may come tomorrow.
Perhaps this longing will lead you to God, Homeland and Love.
Goodbye. Do not forget.'

Korczak's farewell speach to each child on their leaving the orphanage.

Who was this Man?

Janusz Korczak's work with children can only be fully understood within the context of his life.

He was to die as Dr. Henryk Goldszmit, but he was known universally by his pseudonym Janusz Korczak – doctor, writer, educator, philosopher, great humanist and pioneer for the rights of the child, who dedicated his life to helping the destitute and neglected Jewish and Catholic children of Poland. He left as a legacy not only his living and topical educational ideas, in the fields of child psychology and education, but his rich achievements as a writer too – he was the recipient of Poland's highest literary prize, which guaranteed him a permanent place in the history of Polish literature. Korczak's books for children were, and still are, as popular and loved as our *Alice in Wonderland* and *Peter Pan*.

Korczak's convictions and sense of responsibility were so strong, he was prepared to go to his death rather than betray them. A legend was born when, during the Nazi's liquidation of the Warsaw Ghetto, after rejecting countless offers to save himself by his many Polish admirers and friends, he led his two hundred orphans onto the train that would take them to the gas chambers of Treblinka. This man, who had brought up thousands of children, refused to desert them, so that even as they died they would be able to maintain their trust in him and their faith in human goodness.

However, the tragic and heroic death of Janusz Korczak should not be allowed to obscure the richness of his life and the way he lived it – for both sides of the story shine with equal brilliance.

He was born Henryk Goldszmit in Warsaw on 22 July 1879, the descendant of two generations of educated Jews who had broken away from Jewish tradition to assimilate themselves into Polish culture and society. His grandfather was a highly regarded physician, his father an equally successful lawyer. Korczak's early life appeared happy and sheltered, but was shattered at the age of 11 when his father suffered a mental breakdown and had to be institutionalized for the rest of his life. The eventual death of his father, when Korczak was 18, was a severe blow to him and his family, who, having spent most of their savings on the high fees of mental institutions, found that they had no financial means left. They were forced to move from their affluent quarters to a poor district of Warsaw. The next few years proved difficult ones for Korczak. He became the sole bread winner for his mother, grandmother and sister. After studying all day at high school, he would give private lessons to students who needed the extra help. At night he wrote short stories, satires and poems, selling them to a literary weekly newspaper and various other periodicals.

When he was 20 years old, Korczak was awarded first prize in the Paderewsky literary competition – one of the most prestigious in Poland. It was during this period of his life that he took on the pseudonym of 'Janusz Korczak'. On the last day for entering the competition he realized that he had not devised a pen name, as required under the competition's rules. On opening a historical novel by his side he took the name of its hero, Janasz Korczak. A typesetter mistakenly changed 'Janasz' to 'Janusz' – and it stayed that way.

Torn between writing and medicine as a career, it was not through chance that Korczak chose the latter. He wanted to help people, especially the sick and the poor. As he expressed it: 'Writing is only words. Medicine is deeds.' However, Korczak managed successfully to merge both these activities. As a medical student at Warsaw University, he moved to a district of Warsaw stricken by poverty and illiteracy where, in his spare time, he taught children and helped the disadvantaged in any way he could. His first book, *Street Children*, gave a realistic description of his experiences of life in the slums of Warsaw and increased his popularity as a writer. He became involved in the Polish socialist party, but what he learned of their political activity led him to withdraw. He believed in socialism, but only to the extent that it attempted to rectify social injustices, and formed the maxim: 'If you want to reform the world – you must reform education.' When Korczak qualified as a doctor in 1904, he decided to specialize in paediatrics, and started work in the Warsaw Children's Hospital.

A year later Korczak was enlisted as a doctor in the Russian army during the Russian–Japanese War. During his service at the front, where he witnessed the full sufferings and injustices of war, he wrote:

> War is an abomination. Especially because no one reports how many children are hungry, ill-treated and left without protection. Before a nation

goes to war it should stop to think of the innocent children who will be injured, killed or orphaned. No cause, no war is worth depriving children of their natural right to happiness. One must think first of the child before making revolutions.

After the war, Korczak travelled to Berlin, Paris and London to further his medical studies. On his return to Poland, in order to gain a deeper insight into the field of child psychology and behaviour, he accepted the position of supervisor and educator at the Company of Children's Camps, which organized summer holidays for the destitute children of Warsaw. Korczak's experiences in these camps influenced him greatly, and led him to devote more and more time to children's care and education.

Meanwhile, his professional reputation among medical students and educationalists had been growing rapidly. They came from far and wide to attend his lectures. Korczak's personality and methods of teaching can best be illustrated by a lecture he gave at the Institute of Pedagogy in Warsaw, entitled 'The Heart of the Child'. One of his students recalled the event.

> We were all surprised by Korczak's instruction to gather in the X-ray lab. He arrived bringing along a four-year-old boy from the orphanage. The X-ray machine was switched on and we saw the boy's heart beating wildly. He was frightened – so many strange people, darkness in the room, the noise of the machine. Speaking very softly, so as not to add to the child's fears and deeply moved by what could be seen on the

> screen, Korczak told us 'Don't ever forget this sight. How wildly a child's heart beats when he is frightened and this it does even more so when reacting to an adult's anger with him, not to mention when he fears to be punished.' Then heading for the door with the boy's hand in his he added 'That is all for today!' We did not need to be told any more. Everybody will remember that lecture forever.

Korczak was sought after as a physician to the wealthiest families in Warsaw, but he also chose to take care of the children of slum families. He always accepted the 'undesirable' house calls which other physicians refused. His professional fees were high for his wealthy patients, but he treated poor families free of charge, often leaving money to pay for a prescription.

In 1912, in his early thirties, the educator in Korczak emerged victorious over both the doctor and the writer. In later years he explained the reason for this decision. 'A spoon of castor oil is no cure for poverty and parentlessness.' Merely taking care of sick children did not satisfy him, for he realized how helpless medicine was in dealing with social factors. He accepted the position of Director of a new Jewish orphanage, whose well-equipped building, considered one of the most beautiful and advanced in Europe, Korczak personally designed and planned. From then until his death he worked in the orphanage, living in the attic, and receiving no salary.

The only interruption came when he served for four years as a doctor in the Russian army again, during the First World War. It was in the midst of all the bloodshed, at stops on the road and during pauses from treating the wounded and dying soldiers, that Korczak wrote his most important work: *How to Love a Child*. In it he combined his experiences and observations concerning the spiritual and practical nurturing of children, almost as if Kahlil Gibran and Dr. Spock had joined forces. The book could be used as a vehicle to enter the child's mind.

The period between the wars (1918–1939) was a fruitful one for Korczak. The orphanage was an island of happiness for the children in his care compared to others that existed in Poland at that time. Nowhere else were such advanced educational theories and methods being practised. His insights into children were unclouded by sentimentality, but rather based on continuous clinical observation and meticulous recording of data. Neither was he a starry-eyed idealist. He was endowed with an uncanny empathy for children and a deep concern for their rights. He was wise, loving and utterly single minded, without a thought for such things as money, fame, home or family.

In 1922, together with Maryna Falska, a social worker, he set up another orphanage for Catholic children. In both places he employed the same methods and enjoyed the help of dedicated assistants, chief amongst them being Stefania Wilczynska, who worked with him for over 30 years. Korczak was like a father to the children, constantly busy, disappearing and returning, whilst Stefania was a mother figure – the permanent presence. The children could always go to her with the most trivial problems, for she always made time for them. She took care of the orphanage on her own during Korczak's absence at the front, and saved many children during a typhoid epidemic by carrying them to the hospital. The two became the perfect team – Korczak's creativity and imagination were complemented by Stefania's practical abilities.

Side-by-side with his pedagogical activities, Korczak continued to write. In 1923 he published his most famous children's book *King Matt the First*, loved by generations of children and translated into over 20 languages. In it the little prince Matt inherits the crown of a utopian kingdom, and battles against all the injustices of the world, especially those inflicted on children by adults. Children governed, while adults were sent back to school. It is a rare masterpiece of insight on how a child views the world of adults. His other novel, *If I was Small Again*, written around the same time, was half lyrical and half psychological. It told the story of a grown man who turned into a young boy. The reader could thus gain an understanding from an adult's and a child's point of view, making each of them appreciate the other.

However, one of Korczak's most original innovations was the founding of a popular weekly newspaper called *The Little Review*, which he started in 1926. This was produced for and by children. Mailboxes were set up across the country for children to submit questions and problems. 'There will be 12 telephones,' he wrote in the prospectus, 'so that anyone can talk, ask questions or make a complaint at whatever time they want. There will be three editors – one oldster – bald and bespectacled – and two additional editors, a boy and a girl.' The editors, reporters and contributors all received a small salary for their work. Korczak himself rarely wrote for the paper, but every Thursday he presided over a weekly meeting of the newspaper's correspondents. *The Little Review* continued

publication until the outbreak of war in 1939 and was possibly the first venture of its kind in the history of journalism.

Again and again Korczak stressed the importance of respecting the child. Both in theory and practice Korczak was always careful to refrain from any use of his power as an adult. The good educator, he believed, was always seeking to improve and instruct himself in his work. He could learn most from the children themselves. In the orphanage the children came from the harshest and most humiliating backgrounds. They brought with them a wide range of fears, anxieties, distrust and a system of values based on deceit and bluff. Such children lacked the emotional support of a parental figure and as a result were likely to assert themselves on the basis of anti-social norms. Korczak's approach was geared to prevent such a development. First and foremost, he knew that they needed to be able to trust and rely on adults. He, therefore, made it his goal to return to his children the very thing that adult society had deprived them of – respect, love and care.

That Korczak achieved this is revealed by one boy who, on leaving the orphanage, said:

> If not for the home I wouldn't know that there are honest people in the world who never steal. I wouldn't know that one could speak the truth. I wouldn't know that there are just laws in the world.

Korczak had a belief in the innate goodness of children and their natural tendency to improve, given the opportunity and guidance to do so. He felt that childhood was often perceived as a preparation for a future life, when in fact every moment had its own importance – one should appreciate the child for what he or she is and not for what he or she will become. He believed in respecting and understanding the child's own way of thinking instead of perceiving him or her from an adult's point of view. Korczak wrote about this in his many books and articles. He spoke about it at courses in teacher training institutes, and during public lectures and conferences.

Within the orphanage he put his theory into practice when he helped his children to create a 'children's Court' presided over by five child Judges. The Clerk of the Court was a teacher. Every child with a grievance had the right to summon the offender to face the Court of his peers. Teachers and children were equal before the Court – even Korczak had to submit to its judgment. He reported that during one six-month period, he found himself accused six times. He envisaged that within 50 years every school would have its own Court and that they would become a source of liberation for the child, teaching both respect for the law and individual rights.

Every week Korczak would testify in Warsaw's Juvenile Courts, defending the destitute and abandoned street children, who were often given long sentences.

> The delinquent child is still a child. He is a child who has not given up yet, but does not know who he is. A punitive sentence could adversely influence his future sense of himself and his behaviour; it is society that has failed him and made him behave this way.

During the interwar period anti-Semitism increased in Poland. Despite his reputation, even Korczak was affected by it. In 1935 he was engaged as 'The Old Doctor' on Polish State radio, to give talks and answer questions on the subject of children and childcare. The corporation's bosses, who held him in high esteem, did not dare divulge his real name because he was a Jew. Anonymity was the price exacted from him. In a short time his soft, warm, friendly voice, along with his natural humour, won great acclaim all over Poland and acquired an enormous audience. As one child listener reminisced, 'The Old Doctor proved to me for the first time in my life, that an adult could enter easily and naturally into our world. He not only understood our point of view, but deeply respected and appreciated it.'

The editor of the Polish radio magazine *Antena* described Korczak's broadcasts:

> Seemingly he talked to children, but adults were also mesmerized. The Old Doctor emphasized that only love could tie both the young and adults with the world. He was the greatest intellectual and humanist on the Polish radio. He talked with us humbly, quietly, caringly and hesitatingly. He would look at us, watching our suffering, our pain, our poverty and doubts. Seeing and understanding us, but still examining, holding his stethoscope to the heart and the soul and then carefully giving his diagnosis.

As the political conditions in Europe deteriorated, Korczak decided to visit Palestine where some of his former orphans had settled. The pro-Fascist right was on the ascendance. Vigilante groups and anti-Jewish rioters had already appeared on the streets.

Korczak sensed that the Jews of Poland were sitting on a tinderbox. Stefania was already in Palestine – having gone to visit a friend in 1932 she had decided to stay, working in the children's home on a kibbutz. Full of admiration for the commune's educational system, she had urged Korczak to come and see for himself. Her letters awakened his interest and curiosity, and he visited Palestine in the summer of 1934. He was enchanted by the miracles of accomplishment he found there, amazed to see the Jew in the role of the peasant, tilling the soil, making the sterile land fruitful.

> If there is one country where the child is honestly given a chance to express his dreams and his fears, his longings and his perplexions – it is possibly Eretz Yisrael. There a monument should be erected to the unknown

> orphan. The world is not in need of labour and of oranges, as much as it needs a new faith. The faith in future life must be bound up with the child who is the source of all hope. I have not given up hope that I shall be able to spend the last years left to me in Palestine, from where I can always yearn for Poland.

On 1 September 1939 the Germans invaded Poland. A year later the Nazis ordered the Jewish orphanage in Krochamalna Street to relocate to the Jewish ghetto, along with the rest of Warsaw's Jews. Conditions within the ghetto were appalling. Starvation and disease were rampant and the bodies of the dead and dying on the streets became a common sight. Obsessed by a sense of personal responsibility for the survival of his children, even though he was ill and starving himself, Korczak became a 'beggar for the most helpless'. Daily, with a sack thrown over his back, he made his rounds seeking food and medicine for his charges. He felt no constraints in begging people for supplies, sometimes only ending up with a pittance. Committed as he was to the impossible task of caring and providing for his children, Korczak also undertook another truly heroic mission. He agreed to take over what was known as the Orphans' Refuge, used as a temporary hospital for sick and dying children, which he described as 'a mortuary where corpses crawl, run by bandits and thieves who robbed the children of any food or help'. Here he spent all the time he could spare tending to the dying. He arranged for makeshift bunks to be built, so that the children could die with dignity. This was perhaps the first hospice of its kind.

While hunger was growing and disease spreading Korczak still tried to maintain some pretence of normality in the orphanage – teaching, playing and caring for the children. He frequently brought in a new child close to death, whom he had picked up from the street, and whose only salvation was to be taken under his wing. His devoted friends and followers outside the ghetto made countless attempts to persuade him to save his own life. Korczak's reply was always the same: 'You wouldn't abandon your own child in sickness, misfortune or danger, would you? So how can I leave two hundred children now!'

His growing sense of despair made him anxious to leave a final testament. This he did in the form of a diary, which has become almost as famous as *The Diary of Anne Frank*. On the last pages he wrote, 'I am angry with nobody. I do not wish anybody evil. I am unable to do so. I do not know how one can do it.' Up to the last, he lived according to what the rabbinical fathers once wrote: 'When asked, "When everyone acts inhuman, what should a man do?" Their reply was, "He should act more human." ' This is what Korczak did to the very end.

The description of the death march of Korczak and his children on 6 August 1942 has become legendary. They marched with their heads held high, carrying the orphanage flag that Korczak had designed – green with white blossoms on one side and the blue Star of David on the other. As one eye-witness told:

> I will never forget that sight to the end of my life. It was a silent but organized protest against the murderers, a march like which no human eye had ever seen

> before. It was an unbearably hot day. The children went four by four. Korczak went first with his head held high leading a child with each hand. The second group was led by Stefa [who had returned to Poland in 1939, realizing war was inevitable]. They went to their death with a look full of contempt for their assassins. When the ghetto policemen saw Korczak they snapped to attention and saluted. 'Who is that man?' asked the German soldiers. I hid the flood of tears that ran down my cheeks with my hands. I sobbed and sobbed at our helplessness in the face of such murder.

Though weakened by fatigue and undernourishment Korczak walked with a firm step, leading his two hundred children in calm, orderly ranks through the hushed streets of Warsaw to the train station. Without a backward glance he, Stefania and the other teachers helped the neatly dressed children, each carrying a favourite toy or book, up onto the ramps of the waiting freight trucks, whose final destination would be the gas chambers of Treblinka.

*

Marek Jaworski, a highly respected Polish writer and journalist, wrote:

> The bodies of Janusz Korczak and his children were burned. All that is left of them is a handful of ashes and clouds of smoke, which the wind has scattered to the four corners of the earth. However, with this smoke Korczak's ideas circulate around the world – ideas which nothing can destroy or consign to oblivion now.

The Champion of the Rights of the Child

Janusz Korczak spoke of the need for a Declaration of Children's Rights long before the one adopted by the League of Nations in 1924. However, his verdict on the League's effort was less than enthusiastic: 'Their Declaration appeals to goodwill, when it should insist. It pleads for kindness when it should demand.'

In 1959 the United Nations produced its famous Universal Declaration of Human Rights and, not long afterwards, a Second Declaration on the Rights of the Child

(20 November 1959). This was a step forward for children's rights, but as a declaration this new set of principles was not legally binding and did not carry a procedure to ensure its implementation.

When the United Nations declared 1979 'The Year of the Child', it also named it 'The Year of Janusz Korczak' to mark the centenary of his birth. Significantly enough, in that same year it was Poland which proposed that a convention should be drafted based on a text manifestly inspired by the teachings of Korczak. The Polish draft convention proposed, amongst other undertakings, that all children shall be provided with education, social security and health care; shall be protected from exploitation, abuse, torture and the effects of war and, on reaching a reasonable age, shall be consulted on any decisions involving them. This was used as a working basis for the preparation of the final document. The Convention of the Rights of the Child was passed unanimously by the United Nations General Assembly in 1989. It took the world over 50 years to hammer out the 'rights' that Korczak had set out in his books.

In 1993 Thomas Hammarberg, a member of the UN Committee on the Rights of the Child, observed:

> Ten million children die each year as a result of curable diseases and malnourishment. More than one hundred million children are today deprived of primary education. Almost as many are exploited in harmful jobs. Hundreds and thousands of girls and boys are abused in prostitution. Many children are victimised by war. Ten million children are refugees inside or outside

their own country. Millions of disabled children are forgotten or discriminated against. Children are suffering physical violence in their own homes in most of the world.

(*Children in Our Charge: The Child's Right to Resources*, ed. Mary John. Jessica Kingsley Publishers, 1996, p.4)

Korczak's The Rights of the Child

I call for a Magna Charta Libertatis concerning the rights of the child. Perhaps there are more, but I have found these to be the principal rights.

- The child has the right to receive love.
- The child has the right to respect.
- The child has the right to optimal conditions in which to grow and develop.
- The child has the right to live in the present.

- The child has the right to be himself or herself.
- The child has the right to make mistakes.
- The child has the right to fail.
- The child has the right to be taken seriously.
- The child has the right to be appreciated for what he is.
- The child has the right to have secrets.
- The child has the right to *a* lie, *a* deception, *a* theft.
- The child has the right to respect for his possessions and budget.
- The child has the right to education.
- The child has the right to protest an injustice.
- The child has the right to a Children's Court where he can judge and be judged by his peers.

- The child has the right to be defended in the juvenile justice court system.
- The child has the right for respect for his grief.
- The child has the right to commune with God.
- The child has the right to die prematurely.

Recognition of Janusz Korczak

- UNESCO declared 1979 'The Year of the Child'. It also named it 'The Year of Janusz Korczak' to mark the centenary of his birth.
- International Janusz Korczak Associations have been set up worldwide.
- He has been compared to Mother Teresa, Martin Luther King and Socrates.
- Books have been written on his life and educational theories.
- His own writings have been published

and republished in over 20 different languages, including Arabic and Japanese, and his books for children are as famous as *Alice in Wonderland* and *Peter Pan*.

- Germany is currently republishing all his books on education.
- His work is studied at European universities and symposia are devoted to it.
- Andrzej Wajda, Poland's greatest film director, made the film *Korczak*, which was shown worldwide.
- A play *Korczak and his Children* has been performed in many countries.
- Korczak is revered as a saint and martyr.
- Schools, hospitals and streets have been named after him.
- Monuments have been erected to honour him.

- Korczak was posthumously given the German Peace Prize.
- Pope John Paul II said 'For the world today, Janusz Korczak is a symbol of true religion and true morality.'

People are afraid of death because they are not aware of the fact
That such a splendid phenomenon as life can only last a short time.
If it were not so, it would lose its value and we would soon get tired of it.

It is very hard to be born and learn to live.
Ahead of me is a much easier matter – to die.
After death it may be hard again, but I am not bothering about that.
The last year, month or hour, I should like to die consciously in possession of my faculties.
I do not know what I should say to the children by way of farewell.
I should want to make clear to them only this:
That the road is theirs to choose, freely.

The Full Stop! Campaign

The NSPCC (National Society for the Prevention of Cruelty to Children) has launched a huge nation-wide campaign with an aim of truly historic proportions – to end cruelty to children *forever!*

Full Stop! is a year-long awareness and fundraising campaign beginning a sustained initiative to end cruelty to children over a generation. The NSPCC campaign will reach into every home in every village, town and city in the country and aims to raise the issue of stopping child cruelty into *THE* social cause of the Millennium.

Current statistics are stark – each week one child under 5 dies following abuse and neglect; each year an estimated 150,000 children are physically abused; 11 per cent of adults report that they were sexually abused as children.

The NSPCC's campaign and long-term strategy to end cruelty to children has been developed following the National Commission of Inquiry into the Prevention of Child Abuse, which reached a stunning conclusion that '...child abuse and neglect can almost always be prevented – provided the will to do so is there'. Full Stop! is all about ensuring as we progress into a new Millennium that the will will always be there.

The NSPCC's long-term strategy involves five key programme areas dealing with all aspects of the child in society – child protection, quality parenting and family support, education, child-friendly communities and cultural change – achieving a fundamental shift in society's values, attitudes and behaviour towards children. The national Full Stop! appeal for £250 million to fund these new programmes has been launched.

The Full Stop! Campaign has already received huge national support from all walks of life. People across the country are signing a pledge of support to help make ending cruelty to children a reality and there will also be a vast array of events happening all over the country throughout 1999 and 2000.

To find out more about the Full Stop! Campaign and to pledge your support contact: NSPCC, 42 Curtain Road, London EC2 3NH (tel: 0171 825 2500).